MW01608867

a Heart's Window

by LISA SHERK

illustrated by Megan Harrisson

 FriesenPress

 FriesenPress

One Printers Way
Altona, MB R0G 0B0
Canada

www.friesenpress.com

ISBN
978-1-03-918957-7 (Hardcover)
978-1-03-918956-0 (Paperback)
978-1-03-918958-4 (eBook)

1. POETRY, CANADIAN

Distributed to the trade by The Ingram Book Company

Dedication

Forget who you've been and what
you've done.

It's never too late to do what you were
made to do.
Be the story you were made to live.

— Bob Goff

I dedicate this book to the glorious people who surround, love, uplift, and make me the best version of myself.

To my mom, Irene; my son Jacob, daughter-in-law Dawna, and daughter Tessa; my grandchildren Cailee, Beau, and Oak; and my sister-in-law Natalie.

To my dearest friends Barbara and Connie.

To the team of incredible colleagues in the Intensive Care Unit of Niagara Health — Welland site, who I have had the privilege to work beside; especially Bonnie, for the last twenty-five years.

Also, special thanks to Nancy and Megan, without whom this book would not be complete.

Contents

the heartprint

The Heartprint

There is a window to the soul
carried by love, a refuge whole

Heartprints stamped with love, grace
inspired words, healing place

Let others know their worth in life
fiercely infuse hope despite

insecurities, flaws
Show mercy, always love because

our words are like healing rains
They fertilize despairing stains

of hurting, crushed, endless scripts
Instead see worth, leave a heartprint

Display to others what Jesus taught
nailed to a cross, His blood it bought

Forgiveness, faith, second chance
bountiful gardens, seeds that plant

Leaving heartprints upon souls
lost, broken, love's glue beholds

Deep crevices, cracks will mend
a soul's window measures, extends

Show kindness with gestures, words
misled, neglected, shepherds' herds

Blue green beauty, an ocean's glint
mending words leave a heartprint

Build a Dream

She sits at her desk, pen in hand
starts to write, realizes she can
weaves stories, poems
fish swimming upstream
it's never too late to build a dream

Picks up his guitar, starts to strum, sings
words of a song take form on strings
music flows forth
a shining moonbeam
it's never too late to build a dream

Paintbrushes dipped, an oil medium
she feverishly creates
glorious delphiniums
colours are swirling
pink, lavender, cream
it's never too late to build a dream

Picks up his toolbelt, reviewing plans
pounding nails, on a ladder he stands
houses are built
board by board, seam by seam
it's never too late to build a dream

You may be thirteen
or seventy-seven
always believe
reach for stars
in the heavens
remember hopes
you dreamt as a child
when you raced on bikes
jumped off ropes, were wild
believe in gifts
tucked deep in your soul
given to you to create, behold
beautiful colours
yellow, periwinkle, green
it's never too late to build a dream

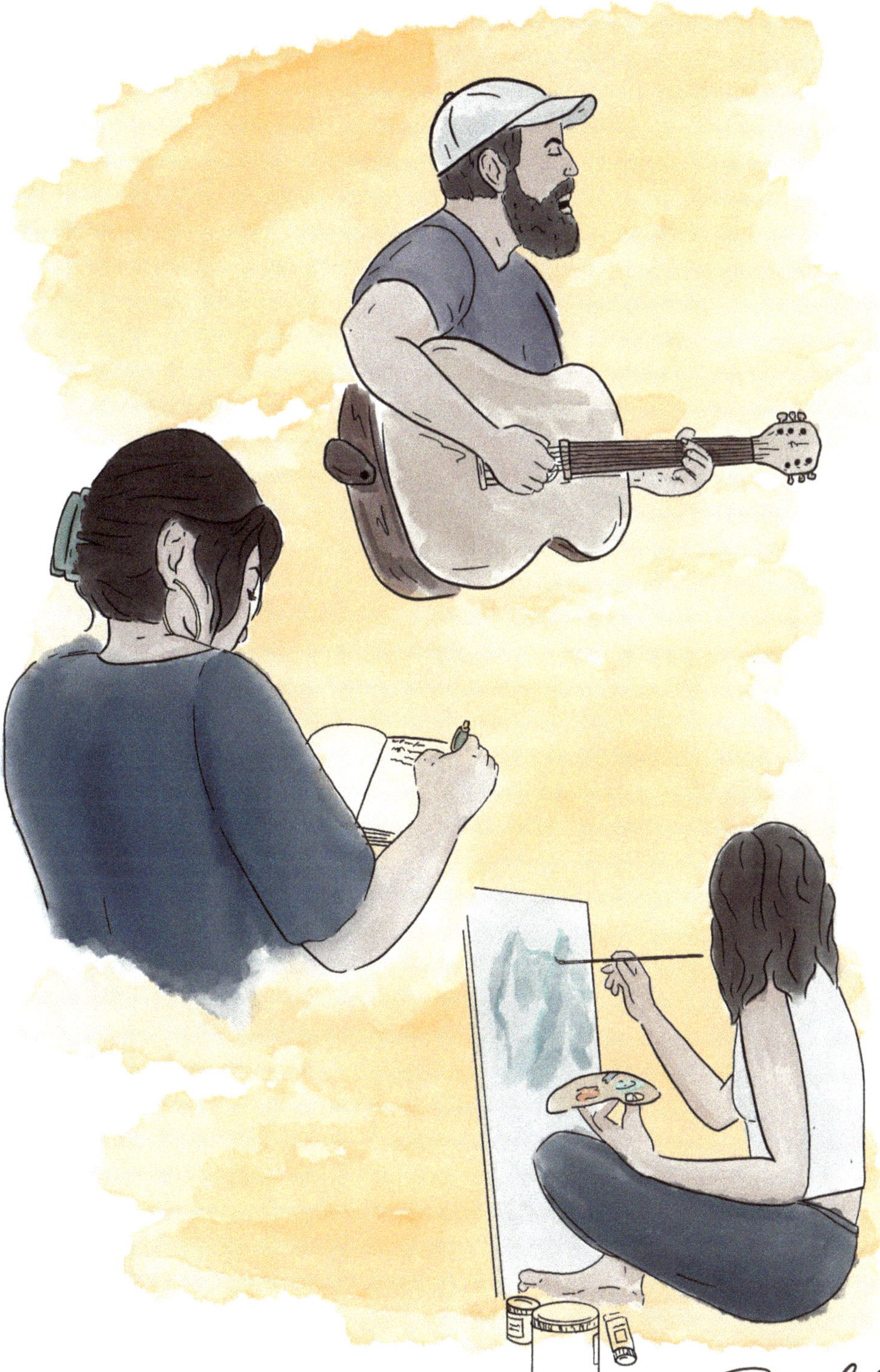

Build a Dream

Mary's House

God gives us gifts
seasons of life
priceless jewels
vivid, dazzling lights

We walk down Walnut
to Oakridge Crescent
view Mary's house
garden's fragrant, pleasant

Friendships given
old, young
Mary eighty-seven
Doug ninety-one

Long winding drive
pass by their chairs
always visits
then down wood stairs

Beach, billowing water
Lake Erie shore
pull out our kayaks
lifejackets, oars

Glide through water
waves rise, swell
sunshine sparkles
colours pastel

Turtles swim
pass by enroute
glorious days
watch him sun, float

Our paddles slice
through clear teal waves
we will cherish these
sunny, August days

They soothe, replenish
tired, weary souls
balmy, warm sunshine
eases our woes

As we near the shore
view Aunt Mary's house
nestled deep on a lot
flowers, gardens boast

Hydrangeas, roses
rhododendrons bloom
Doug, Mary's gifts
shovels, rubber boots

An unlikely friendship
blooms like Mary's garden
between young, old souls
all the years there are none

Thankful for these gifts
Doug, Mary's house
as we wave down the lane
smiles in our hearts

Mary's house

Cottage Music

Rolling waves, whitecaps I view
purple martins, wings of blue

Lake house sounds
orchestra lyrics
percussion, strings
cottage music

Crunching sounds of feet on stone
walkers with a love to roam

Lifted hands, bicycle traffic
harmonies,
cottage music

Crashing waves
that pound, spray
against rocks, sunny days

Children in lakes, who frolic
glee, laughter
cottage music

An ice cream cone, drips delicious
family meals, clearing dishes

Crackling fires, guitars poetic
on lawn chairs singing
cottage music

Kayaks gliding, smooth on water
sun glistens, diamonds
beside my daughter

Hinges that slam, screen doors rustic
I sigh, contentment
cottage music

Thankful for this gift in time
cherishing all that is mine

Revelling in summer magic
immersed in sounds
cottage music

Cottage Music

The Garden Party

Edison bulbs, fairy lights

hung from branches, starlit nights

ladies, friends

walk on cobblestone

lanterns hung, worries postponed

tables adorned

antique plates, cups

party dresses on each of us

as violin music floats through the air

rest, this moment

lay worries, cares

saturated beauty, friends sublime

an August evening, summertime

dahlias, zinnias

hydrangeas white

conversing, laughter, smiles, delight

gifts are given

Connie's garden party

we feast on food, delicious, hearty

under twinkling stars

as crickets sing

hearts full of love

music, violin strings

moments in time, priceless gold

women surround me

hands to hold

a garden party

beneath fairy lights

our hearts o'erflow

this August night

Garden Party

Lisa Sherk — 13

Layers of Memories

I close my eyes
sounds of home
rippling waves as rivers flow

Layers of memories
summer, sand
wash over, fill me
replenish, expand

Feelings of yesteryear
simpler times
my hand in Grandpa's
smile lines

From his eyes such wisdom
flowed as he spoke
layers of memories
feelings evoke

Running barefoot
on dew-filled grass
racing on bicycles
hopes surpassed

I close my eyes; sounds of home
glisten like raindrops
on windows alone

Layers of memories
bring me to tears
fathomless moments
of earlier years

Sounds of my children
their little hands
clasped tightly in mine
vacations planned

As layers of memories
wash over me
gratitude flowing
in this life's journey

layers of
memories

The Place I Love

The place I love

is next to you

holding your hand

water's aqua hue

coffee with

dearest friends

winding paths

a camera lens

comfy chairs

grandchildren tucked

under my arm

with love

awestruck

tables with

my family set

meals enjoyed

their silhouettes

walks along

lake's

cornflower waves

seagulls shout

my mind creates

next to me

my daughter walks

laughter as

we smile, talk

no need for more

of finer things

serenity

a full heart brings

this beauty right

in front of me

autumn leaves

red, yellow, green

views of nature

sparrows' wings

love for children

flows, wellsprings

gaze toward

heaven above

submerged, surrounded

the place I love

the Place
I love

Thirteen Years

On August thirteenth

       two thousand nine

my blue-eyed blonde girl

       was finally time

An arrival, gift

       beautiful girl

full of life, bright smiles

       bouncy blonde curls

For thirteen years

       every minute, day

your wonderful heart

       kindness that stays

How do I measure

       how much you are loved

deeper than oceans

       stars twinkling above

Higher than mountains

       wider than sapphire seas

forever I'll love you

       my Cailee, Rosie

thirteen
years

Masterpiece

I hope you know
the masterpiece

you are to those
you love with ease

intensely shining
as emeralds green

kindness o'erflows
rippling streams

I hope you know
the masterpiece

your healing hands
a gentle breeze

kindness, always
you express

compassion and
a quiet sense

people surround you
as moths to flames

quick-witted humour
laughter proclaimed

more than autumn leaves
yellow, orange, red

beaming sunshine
an embroidered thread

I hope you know
what lies beneath

magnificent colours
a masterpiece

Masterpiece

An Empty Day

A day without your hand in mine
laughter and your smiling eyes

Is like a bird that doesn't sing
cannot fly, flutter its wing

Long dialogues, stories told
moments cherished
'til we grow old

Beside you I will always stay
without you is
an empty day

Each morning as my sleep abates
open my eyes your heart awaits

Its kindness
overwhelms me still
smoothes all cracks
crevices fill

Fishing boats on waves that sway
blowing winds, gentle rains

Trilling songs, nightingale's display
without you is
an empty day

Reflections of life that's past
winding roads, twisting paths

Thunderous clouds
illuminating sunshine
dark, winter years
no longer mine

Rather, moments, days are full
the hush of silence
your tender soul

More than sand
on beaches that lay
without you is
an empty day

an empty day

Every Detail

Every detail

imprinted, stamped

upon my soul

this love I have

Each moment

every second, day

joy I feel

seeing your face

Depths of wonder

beauty resides

inside your heart

such love abides

Its kindness

inundates me still

each dream

we share

begins, fulfills

Every detail

I cherish, adore

carry your heart

you have restored

in me, such joy

crystalline seas

jagged edges

smoothed, uncreased

I'll cherish, love

hold your hand

what's left, this life

with you, I'll stand

Laugh, cry, dance, sing

every detail

my everything

Etched, engrained

upon my heart

always, forever

is where we'll start

every detail

Still

I believe in fairytales
although my life has not
been filled with princes, honesty
often life's been fraught
disappointment, failure
splintered hopes
vanquished dreams
I believe, someday my cup
will overflow at the seams
still...

I believe there's someone
who will hold my hand each day
we'll grow old together
clasp every word I say
though I peer through windows
glance at narratives told
I'll keep a space
in my heart
until such dreams unfold
still...

I believe in kindness
there are people in this life
who fill each day with sunshine
being with them
garners smiles
days spent with my family
no better way I know
others glance through dormers
see my life, a fairytale
still...

Someday I'll look back
at the gift of life I've had
minutes, moments, days well spent
trials I withstand
are there to soften edges
make me kinder, eyes to see
every ounce of magic
dreams are waiting
there for me
still...

Still

Blow a Kiss

Blow a kiss, put it in your pocket
remember me
pictures seen, a locket

Occasions that
we spent in time
nurtured, captured
this heart of mine

Blow a kiss, put it in your pocket
pictures of me
such joy skyrockets

Millions of memories
laughter, tears
I'll cherish, treasure
minutes, years

Given to me
life's precious gifts
are recollected
on waters drift

Blow a kiss, put it in your pocket
movie screens
of Paris markets

Each moment, inkling
priceless jewels
life goes on
restored, refuels

Blow a kiss, put it in your pocket
if I miss you
I will make deposits

From my memory bank
every picture clear
kaleidoscopes
it's your face that sears

Blow a kiss; put it in your pocket
close my eyes
fireworks, a comet

Remember you
hold visions close
never far from me
I love you the most

Blow
a kiss

Blanket of Snow

November Sunday

blanket of snow

shrouds the ground

chipmunks in tow

dustings of snow, evergreen boughs

cardinals' wings, upon the brow

of cottages by waters, shores

porch swing, sunroom

fireplace, stone

steaming coffee, journal in hand

blankets of snow

from window's glanced

branches rustle

winds gently blow

fulfillment rooted

in my soul

memories of storms

darkest nights

passing hope, promise, light

sparkling sunshine, overlays snow

assurance of spring

midst winds that blow

quiet Sunday morning

introspection, rest

fresh blanket of snow

assuredly blessed

Blanket of Snow

Things That Matter

Things that matter
family close

Walks along
lakes that flow

Laughter, my
grandchildren's hands

Concealed in mine
game nights planned

Forest walks on trails that bend
white pages fresh
with words I pen

Snowflakes fall, carpet of snow
toques, mittens
snowballs thrown

Christmas trees with fairy lights
bowls of popcorn, movie nights

Piping cider, hot chocolate
things that matter
my favourite

Treasures stored deep in my heart
memories made
they ne'er depart

Things that matter
cost little yet
the impact great
love is met

things that
Matter

Lisa Sherk — 43

Lengthen Your Table

She sits in her chair
nursing home address
waits for children
no visits amass
her memories, a lifetime
now far from reach
alone with thoughts
wipes tears from her cheeks

He stands at corners
sign in his hand
wrong turns, poor choices
hungry he stands
addiction has taken
him deeper, yet still
he yearns for a life
to be free, fulfilled

Perhaps we could lengthen
our tables this year
look past all the bustle,
gifts that appear
reach out our hands
to neighbours in need
a family that's struggling
children to feed

Visit the elderly who've given so much
gently hold hands
with the lonely
and touch
hearts that are hurting
struggling this year
let's lengthen our tables
show grace, adhere

To the meaning of Christmas
as shepherds they came
followed the star
to the Saviour, His name
heals all hurts
brokenness, mends

Let's lengthen our tables

this Christmas

Amen.

Lengthen your table

Broken

She lifts her head
his side of the bed
echoes of love
now abandoned promises

Tears falling down
saturate lashes
storybook endings
waves against rocks, crashes

Moments, trips
holding hands
with their son
house built on sand
all coming undone

Holidays, birthdays
celebrations
have been tossed
in the sea
for another woman

Deliberate choices
decisions were made
family, home
love she gave

Now fractured, splintered
glass thrown on floors
memories, love
this man she adored

She lifts her head
his side of the bed
draws in breath
exhales gently
she is determined

Strong, courageous
beautiful woman
mama to her son
keeper, all she's been given

Closes her eyes in prayer
strength for each day she asks
lifts her face, warm sun
in this moment, hopes amass

Whispered pleas,
all that's stolen
tears fall fresh
on her cheeks
although her heart's eroding
a mantra she repeats

She is brave, resilient
love deep as an ocean
with time, forgiveness
she'll no longer be broken

Broken

Mosaic

The beauty of
a severed life,
failed promises
darkest night,

Though storms rage on
as shadows fill
I'll rest, my heart
steadfast, be still

Pick up shattered
pieces, glass
make mosaics
trials pass

In its wake
a masterpiece
collage of beauty
pain released

As lapping waves
on oceans flow
clasping beauty
my placated soul

Remember still
God knows all
picks up the fragments
as pieces fall

Weaves, mends
mosaics made
as beauty shines
artists create

No matter all
the times we break
brokenness,
mosaics make

Mosaic

Who I Am

Who I am
are hazel eyes
love of turquoise
never disguised

Treacherous paths
valleys low
radiant sunshine
life ebbs, flows

Failures, triumphs
whispered pleas
resilience, faith
these are keys

Knowing that my story brings
to others hope,
voices that sing

Gray hair, wrinkles
saggy skin
yet thankful
every day I'm in

Challenged always
to improve
how I love
kindness I choose

Who I am
are valleys, streams
promise, heartache
lakes, dreams

Mother, daughter
grandma, friend
nurse, beach-glasser
love that transcends

More than I could have hoped for

this life such beauty

an opened door

that I've walked through

such joy sublime

who I am

is this...defined

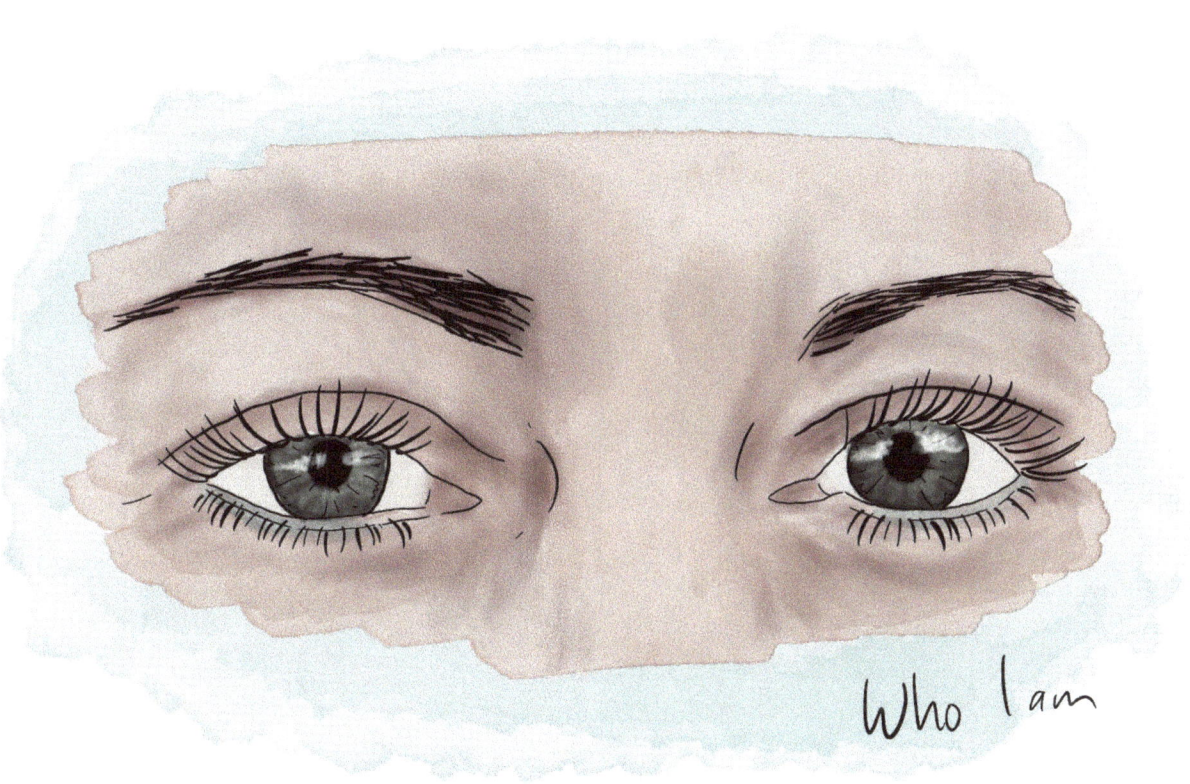

Who I am

Forgotten Dreams

He's not forgotten all your dreams
though storms rage fierce
waters careen

Heartbreak sits
beside you still
as teardrops fall
darkness fills

Amidst your fear that rests beside
it holds your hand as silence hides

Sun will shine
birds will sing
brokenness will
not reign king

Cracks that fill your heart today
will mend once more
like waves that spray

Against sandy shores of lakes
erases, eases your heartbreak

Dreams are still yours to keep
wipe away each
tear that seeps

Believe in every desire you've stored
deep in your heart as music soars

Your dreams are not
forgotten, lost
unsteady paths
steep mountains cost

Prices we pay, lessons learned
my faith holds strong
know this for sure

Amidst the pain, uncertainty
He's not forgotten all your dreams

Forgotten dreams

As Grief Takes Hold

Eras of life

where time collides

grief takes hold

it's not polite

rains that pour

drench, enfold

churn over you

as grief takes hold

disfigured dreams

disintegrate

like splintered wood

bones that break

assurances lost

tumbled autumn leaves

plummet, descend

from old oak trees

once again

like stories told

dig deep, believe

as grief takes hold

each step proceed

teardrops fall

moisten, cleanse

your grief that calls

in time, release

though pain resides

life will go forth

exquisite lines

bruises, scars

regenerate

will mend your pain

alleviate

months, years

chapters unfold

embrace with warmth

as grief lets go

As grief
takes hold

Thankful

Thankful for
arms that swim
hold paddles as
I'm kayaking,
slicing through
green azure lakes
hands that hold
fragrant bouquets

Thankful for
legs that walk
along lakes
as seagulls flock

Eyes that gaze
upon views
lapping waves
glistening blue

These ears that hear
sounds of songs,
music that plays
guitar strings drawn

This heart that beats
a strong muscle,
as children laugh
play, tousle

Thankful for
fingers, hands
that play piano
the bench that stands
as music flows
crescendos clear
often brings
me close to tears

Although I've aged
my body size
is different through
the years, time
wrinkles and
some smile lines
I've laughed, cried,
loved, divine

Thankful every
moment, day
I am alive, unafraid
I'll cherish every
minute spent
with family, friends
I am content
as I age, look different
thankfulness, in this moment

thankful

You Matter to Me

Each stone he lays
created beauty
gifted hands
you matter to me
artistry, what I see
in mortar, bricks
you matter to me
needles, yarn
as she crochets
her piano
each key she plays
a voice that sings
to me, so pleasing
she is a gift
you matter to me
his curly hair
twinkling eyes
imagination, how time flies
they run, play
each unique
precious grandsons
you matter to me
she makes me laugh
her tender heart
a wonder that
sets her apart
she's grown up
time is a thief
I hope you know
you matter to me
each of us
needs to be seen
demands to feel
noticed, perceived
young or old
ages between
each heart that beats

you matter to me
though stained, scarred
with battle wounds
her voice still sings
beautiful tunes
healing will come
in small degrees
cracks, attenuate
you matter to me

You Matter
to Me

Lisa Sherk — 71

Bouquets of Beautiful

In this life of bends, turns
bouquets of beautiful
whilst lessons learned

Sadness, sorrow rears its face
bouquets of beautiful
reach out, embrace

Pathways often
steeped with curves
yet moments held
views superb

Failure cannot rest for long
bouquets of beautiful
shrouded in song

Believing, deepest
faith always
although dark clouds
nay, sunny days

Bouquets of beautiful
simple things
such joy, my faith
to that, I'll cling

Push, deflated
heartbreak past
bouquets of beautiful
this I have

Slip on boots
raincoat adorns
collect beachglass
amongst rose thorns

Grasp belief
hope conveyed
bouquets of beautiful
a heart's ballet

Bouquets of Beautiful

About the Author

LISA SHERK has been a critical care registered nurse in the Intensive Care Unit for 37 years. She is the author of *The Looking Glass (2022)* and is presently working on further projects. As another outlet of her creative expression, Lisa composes songs, singing, and playing piano. She has two beautiful children, three grandchildren, and lives in Port Colborne, Ontario.

About the Illustrator

MEGAN HARRISSON has been painting and drawing since early childhood. Now a critical care registered nurse with a passion for both healthcare and the visual arts, she creates both personally inspired work and creative commissions utilizing paint on canvas, watercolour paint, linework, and digital design. This love for creativity and exploration of varying concepts, styles, and medium brings opportunity to align and understand others' perspectives and emotions to be translated into her artwork. Illustrations for these poems have been created through close collaboration to translate the emotions and feelings of the author, the reader, and those who have inspired the carefully stitched, heart-felt words.

Printed in the USA
CPSIA information can be obtained
at www.ICGtesting.com
JSHW072033091123
51750JS00005B/11